AF450038

POPE FRANCIS

TO HEAL THE WORLD

Catechesis on the pandemic

Preface by
Cardinal Peter Kodwo Turkson

PREFACE

The Occasion

The days from the 21ˢᵗ to the 26ᵗʰ of March 2020 were the period of Italy's worst affliction by the Covid-19 virus. When on 27 March Pope Francis, defying the rain, climbed alone onto the tribune of St. Peter's Square to preside over a special prayer service to end a Covid-19 virus infection that had become a global pandemic, he resembled the *suffering servant of God* in the prophecy of Isaiah (*Is.* 52:13-53:12), bearing the brokenness, pain and the bewilderment of humanity which was afflicted and terrorized by a virus it knew little about, and for whose infection it had no remedy. He expressed the collective anxiety of the world thus: "*The storm exposes our vulnerability and uncovers those false and superfluous certainties around which we have constructed our daily schedules, our projects, our habits, and priorities*".[1]

At prayer on the tribune, Pope Francis also fulfilled the image of the *high priest (Heb*

---

[1] POPE FRANCIS, *Extraordinary Moment of Prayer,* 27 March 2020.

5: 1) who represented the human family before God and not only brought to God its collective pain and anxiety, but also sought from God healing and consolation: God, *"the Father of mercies and the God of all consolation"* was consoling him in his affliction, so that he mzay be able to *"to console those who are in any affliction with the consolation"* with which he is consoled by God (cf. *2Cor.* 1:3-4). And the *Catechesis* which follow represent Pope Francis serving humanity as a *consoler* and a *counselor*, indicating pathways to travel in these Covid-19 times.

During the pontificates of Pope Francis and his predecessor, Pope Benedict XVI, our world has and continues to weather the storms of three (3) crises: the financial crisis of 2008-2009 during the pontificate of Pope Benedict XVI, and the current twin crises of the Climate Change and Covid-19 virus. Crises are defining moments that bring challenges, but also opportunities. Accordingly, Pope Francis exhorts us not to come out of a crisis the same way we entered it. He exhorts us to *"regenerate"* and to *"prepare the future"*! And if we ask: what we may do with a crisis, like the Covid-19 virus, and how *prepare the future,* Pope Benedict XVI helps provide a direction. He said about the financial crisis of 2008, *"The current crisis obliges us to re-plan our journey, to set ourselves new rules and to discover new forms of commitment, to build on positive experiences and to reject negative ones. The crisis thus becomes an opportunity for discernment, in which to shape a new vision for the future. In this spirit, with confidence rather than resignation, it is appropriate to address the difficulties of the present time"*.[2]

Healing the World

In his *catechesis* during the Wednesday public audiences in late August and throughout September 2020, Pope Francis sought to address to the Church and the world with words of consolation and to propose inspiring alternatives to former lifestyles, habits and social structures which the pandemic has shown deficient in equality and justice, unsustainable and needing drastic reform to uphold the central value of the human person. The *normality* to which the Pope would like us to aspire after, as missionary disciples, is anticipating on earth, with our actions, policies and decisions, God's Kingdom of justice, peace and equality among brothers and sisters

---

[2] POPE BENEDICT XVI, *Caritas in Veritate* [CV], 21. (Emphasis is mine)

who have one God as a Father. Thus, in order to prefigure a more just, inclusive and a sustainable world that can better pull us through the onslaught of the Covid-19 pandemic, the Pope invites us to join him on a new *journey*. It is *a pilgrimage* that is inspired by the Gospel of Christ, our Saviour and healer, and which has, as beacons, the theological virtues, *faith, hope* and *charity*: namely, the *certainty of our faith* in God, the creator of all things and Lord of history, the *generous offer of God's love in Christ* to us and the *assurance of hope in his promises*. It is, therefore, also *a pilgrimage* of life that is lived in the Church, as the "*Charity of Christ*" and which illumines our conduct, actions and decision-making in economics, politics, ecology and healthcare etc., and whose application to life-issues over the years and in dialogue with human sciences and traditional wisdom has engendered the "*Principles of the social teaching of the Church*".[3]

Using the compositional style, made popular by Cardinal Cardijn: "*see, judge* and *act*", each *catechesis* begins with an announcement of a theme, followed by an exposé (*see*). Then, with reference to the Scriptures (attrib-

---

[3] *Compendium of the Social Doctrine of the Church* [*CSDC*], Ch. 4.

utes of the Kingdom of God and/or the virtues of *faith, hope* and *charity*), the sense of the theme is explored (*judge*). Finally, and with reference to the *Church's social Doctrine*, an application of the theme is presented (*act*). An invitation to action or an intercessory prayer about the theme concludes the *catechesis.*

The Pope's invitation to *journey* together along the path of healing a Covid-19 stricken world and discerning the future is addressed to all. For, the experience that the human family is making of Covid-19 is neither local, national nor regional. It is a global pandemic that lays bare the fragility of human existence and, so, evokes our sense of inter-dependence and inter-relatedness. Discerning the path of healing and recovery through this pandemic is certainly not a thing for *"lone rangers"*. It is a global venture that does not admit individualism, whether it is personal or collective, whether it is expressed in the form of political nationalisms or economic vested interests. Neither do our global efforts allow indifference nor *"lookers on from the balcony"*. The way to exit from the crisis as better human beings, living in healthier societies is a *common venture.* It is through *communion* and with a special attention to the weakest, the poor and creation.

The Catechesis

The introductory *catechesis* presents Jesus as the healer and *"the apostle of our faith"* (*Heb*. 3:1). Jesus' healing reveals the Kingdom of God, which in turn inaugurates an era of grace, of which the first signs are the spiritual gifts of *faith, hope* and *charity.* These spiritual gifts dispose us (people) for God's consolation and healing. Furthermore, they do not only equip us to bring solace and healing to the afflicted (*2Cor*. 1:3-5), but they also make us agents of transformation of *"the roots of our physical, spiritual and social infirmities and destructive practices…"* and builders of a *civilization of love*.

The second *catechesis* and occasion for healing opens with an observation of how the pandemic has shown humanity vulnerable, but inter-connected, and the need to care for its poor and the earth. The vulnerability of the person reflects other social ills that need to be healed, principally, the appreciation of the value and character of the human person under such negative conditions. With our gaze still strained on Jesus, we learn that just as the shameful death of Jesus on the cross did not prevent the centurion from recognizing in him *"the Son of God"* (*Mk*. 15:39), so must the frailty of the human condition, exposed by

Covid-19 not becloud our vision of the splendour of both human nature and its vocation/destiny even in victims of Covid-19. For, not only is the human person a *relational being;* but to believe in God, the Father who loves all men and women with an infinite love means to realize that *"God thereby confers upon them an infinite dignity"*.[4] Dignity, as the supreme endowment of the human person, makes us all *common: brothers and sisters* (adelphoi = a-delphoi) from the same womb and, therefore, equal in dignity. Neither Covid-19 nor State policy can diminish one's dignity; and people may not be treated dismissively or denied access to healthcare. Rather, this is time to appreciate all healthcare givers who risk life to uphold value of life and others' dignity.

Following up on the healing of relationships in the previous *catechesis,* the third *catechesis* is an occasion to heal a social ill, exposed by the pandemic, namely, "social injustice", in the forms of *inequality, marginalization* and *discrimination* etc., and to recall the principle of *"the preferential option for the poor"*. This principle is, in fact, a Gospel imperative, according to which all *"are called to be instrument of God for the liberation and promotion of*

---

[4] POPE FRANCIS, *Evangelii Gaudium* [EG], 178.

the poor in society".[5] Poverty can be a deeply spiritual attitude before God from whom one receives everything, as gift. Thus, it can be an expression of one's dignity before the God of love. When, however, the pandemic or any other condition in society hurts one's dignity, making him/her less free and human, and, therefore, poor, such poverty needs to be avoided or resisted, together with the pandemic itself and all other *"social pandemics"* which cause it. The return to *normality* cannot include these *social pandemics*. They must be healed, as the Covid-19 pandemic itself. Jesus who became poor, making himself the servant of all, left his followers an example and a legacy of *loving service: "You must wash one another's feet"* (*Jn.* 13:14). That is how the epidemics of social injustice are healed!

Loving service generates *hope* and *hopefulness* that can heal the gross inequalities uncovered by the pandemic. Thus, the fourth *catechesis* is an occasion to heal these injustices through the principle of the universal destination of the goods. As a "fruit of unequal economic growth" which disregards the primacy of the person, his or her dignity and wellbeing in all activities, as well as the wellbeing of

---

[5] *Ibid.*, 187.

the *common home,* inequality of any sort in the world is contrary to God's design in creation. When, however, *"tilling and keeping"* (*Gen.* 2:15) become a *loving service* (stewardship/ care/ administration= *oikonomia*) to the earth, her good things are shared and are *destined to serve the wellbeing of all* (*Acts* 4:32-35): in the present generation, future generations and of the earth herself.

The fifth *catechesis* is an occasion to heal our brokenness, through a conversion of our natural belongingness and inter-relatedness into a virtue of *solidarity* in Christ.[6] Every person created by God, loved and saved in Christ, fulfils himself/herself by creating a network of multiple relationships of love, justice and solidarity with other persons.[7] This natural consequence of our nature, as relational beings, living in a living network of relationships to support and help one another, is also revealed in these Covid-19 times to be vulnerable. There is talk about the poor suffering most, minorities dying most, loneliness and suicides, psychological depressions, no shipment of health equipment outside certain regions, the appropriation of technolo-

---

[6] Cf. SAINT POPE JOHN PAUL II, *Sollicitudo rei socialis* [*SRS*], 38-40.
[7] *CSDC*, Ch. 4; 35.

gies and vaccines by countries etc. We have been selfish, individualistic and indifferent, and have not watched over each other well enough! Our *Solidarity "presumes the creation of a new mindset which thinks in terms of community and the priority of the life of all over the appropriation of goods by a few".* [8]

The sixth *catechesis* deals with healing our world and society generally from negative personal, social and political national sentiments of vain competition, rivalry, hatred, lack of cooperation, indifference and individualism through the nurturing of a *civilization of love* that promotes the *common good* on all levels. Love, likened to light, is considered the first act of God's creation. As love of God and love of neighbour, it is the fulfilment of God's covenant with his people; and Jesus makes it the distinguishing mark of his followers. Indeed, in the *Beatitudes* (*Lk* 6:27-36), Jesus teaches his disciples to put others first out of love. Such love unarms bigotry, competition, rivalry, hatred and dissensions: sentiments which militate against the pursuit of the *common good,* as the *"guarantee of personal, familial and associative good".*[9] And since *"every Chris-*

---

[8] *Ibid.,* 188.
[9] *CSDC,* 61.

tian is called to practise this charity , in a manner corresponding to his vocation and according to the degree of influence he wields in the polis",[10] none is exempt from pursuing and contributing to the *common good.*

The previous *catechesis* had dealt mostly with our relationship with God and with human beings (their conduct, society, structures and institutions etc.). This seventh *catechesis* is the occasion to heal our relationships with creation through contemplation. Indeed, the first charge that was bestowed on the human person at creation was to *"till and to keep"* its garden-home. *"Tilling"* ensured the person of her feed. But, *"keeping"* ensured that the garden-home remained a garden: a place of attention and care. *"Keeping"* or *"care"* then, entail a responsibility towards the *garden-home* (creation), which has not been easy to keep. The violence that is present within the human heart reflects on it;[11] and human treatment of creation has been described as *sinful.*[12] By way of healing this relationship and enabling the person and society to fulfil her responsibility towards creation, the *catechesis* invites to *contemplation*: to recognize the creator of

---

[10] CV, 7.
[11] POPE FRANCIS, *Laudato si'* [LS], 2.
[12] *Ibid.,* 8.

all things (Cf. *Ps.* 19), his design for all things and his bestowal of all things on the human person, as *gift,* and to be grateful, rejoice and celebrate!

A healing of our Covid-19 stricken world that is whole and wholesome must be the task of all; and so the eighth *catechesis* is an occasion to underline the great urgency and necessity that all must be helped to be able to contribute to, to own and to be responsible for the healing process. If *solidarity* meant that the healing of our world must be a joint-effort: all acting together to heal the world, then *subsidiarity* recognizes that in certain cases, people must be helped (given assistance = *subsidium*) and enabled to participate in and to contribute to this joint effort. When it is the State that helps people to play their role, the State simply props up people to become protagonists of their required roles and responsibilities towards the healing of our world, its institutions and its structures: in sum to fashion a better world.

The final *catechesis* concludes the senses on healing a Covid-19 stricken world, announces a new *journey* for a new future, with our gaze still fixed on Christ, our healer. Jesus' healing is whole and wholesome. All aspects of the person and all areas of life are affected.

Jesus now sends us forth to do likewise: to heal victims of Covid-19 virus and to heal our society of all that make it less human. For, the God who consoles us in all our afflictions now sends us forth as consolers of those who are in any affliction (cf. *2Cor.* 1:3-5), and in his Spirit to renew the face of the earth!

Cardinal PETER KODWO TURKSON
Prefect of the Dicastery
for Promoting Integral Human Development

TO HEAL THE WORLD

Catechesis on the pandemic

INTRODUCTION

Dear brothers and sisters, good morning!

The pandemic continues to cause deep wounds, exposing our vulnerability. On every continent there are many who have died, many are ill. Many people and many families are living a time of uncertainty because of socio-economic problems which especially affect the poorest.

Thus, we must keep our gaze firmly fixed on Jesus (see *Heb* 12:2): in the midst of this pandemic, our eyes on Jesus; and with this *faith* embrace the *hope* of the Kingdom of God that Jesus Himself brings us (see *Mk* 1:5; *Mt* 4:17).[1] A Kingdom of healing and of salvation that is already present in our midst (see *Lk* 10:11). A Kingdom of justice and of peace that is manifested through works of *charity*, which in their turn increase hope and strengthen faith (see *1 Cor* 13:13). Within the Christian tradition, *faith, hope and charity* are much more than feelings or attitudes. They are virtues infused in us through the grace of the Holy Spirit:[2] gifts that heal us

---

[1] See *Catechism of the Catholic Church* [CCC], 2816.
[2] *Ibid.*, 1812, 1813.

and that make us healers, gifts that open us to new horizons, even while we are navigating the difficult waters of our time.

Renewed contact with the Gospel of faith, of hope and of love invites us to assume a creative and renewed spirit. In this way, we will be able to transform the roots of our physical, spiritual and social infirmities and the destructive practices that separate us from each other, threatening the human family and our planet.

Jesus's ministry offers many examples of healing: when He heals those affected by fever (see *Mk* 1:29-34), by leprosy (see *Mk* 1:40-45), by paralysis (see *Mk* 2:1-12); when He restores sight (see *Mk* 8:22-26; *Jn* 9:1-7), speech or hearing (see *Mk* 7:31-37). In reality, He heals not only the physical evil — which is true, physical evil — but He heals the entire person. In that way, He restores the person back to the community also, healed; He liberates the person from isolation because He has healed him or her.

Let's think of the beautiful account of the healing of the paralytic at Capernaum (see *Mk* 2:1-12) that we heard at the beginning of the audience. While Jesus is preaching at the entrance to the house, four men bring their paralyzed friend to Jesus. Not being able to enter because there was such a great crowd there, they make a hole in the roof and let the stretcher down in front of Him. Jesus who was preaching sees this stretcher coming down in front of Him. "When Jesus saw their faith, he said to the paralytic, 'Child, your sins are forgiven' " (v. 5). And then, as a visible sign, He adds: "Rise, pick up your mat, and go home" (v. 11).

What a wonderful example of healing! Christ's action is a direct response to the faith of those people, to the hope they put in Him, to the love they show that they have for each other. And so, Jesus heals, but He does not simply heal the paralysis. Jesus heals everyone, He forgives sins, He renews the life of the paralyzed man and his friend. He makes him born again, let's say it that way. It is a physical and spiritual healing, all together, the fruit of personal and social contact. Let's imagine how this friendship, and the faith of all those present in that house, would have grown thanks to Jesus's action, that healing encounter with Jesus!

And so we can ask ourselves: today, in what way can we help heal our world? As disciples of the Lord Jesus, who is the physician of our souls and bodies, we are called to continue "His work, work of healing and salvation"[3] in a physical, social and spiritual sense.

---

[3] *Ibid.*, 1421.

Although the Church administers Christ's healing grace through the Sacraments, and although she provides healthcare services in the remotest corners of the planet, she is not an expert in the prevention or the cure of the pandemic. She helps with the sick, but she is not an expert. Neither does she give specific socio-political pointers.[4] This is the job of political and social leaders. Nevertheless, over the centuries, and by the light of the Gospel, the Church has developed several social principles which are fundamental,[5] principles that can help us move forward in preparing the future that we need. I cite the main ones which are closely connected: the principle of the dignity of the person, the principle of the common good, the principle of the preferential option for the poor, the principle of the universal destination of goods, the principle of the solidarity, of subsidiarity, the principle of the care for our common home. These principles help the leaders, those responsible for society, to foster growth and also, as in the case of the pandemic, the healing of the personal and social fabric. All of these principles

---

[4] See St Paul VI, Apostolic Letter *Octogesima adveniens* [OA], 14 May 1971, no. 4.
[5] See *CSDC*, 160-208.

express in different ways the virtues of faith, hope and love.

In the next few weeks, I invite you to tackle together the pressing questions that the pandemic has brought to the fore, social ills above all. And we will do it in the light of the Gospel, of the theological virtues and of the principles of the Church's social doctrine. We will explore together how our Catholic social tradition can help the human family heal this world that suffers from serious illnesses. It is my desire that everyone reflect and work together, as followers of Jesus who heals, to construct a better world, full of hope for future generations.[6] Thank you.

General Audience, 5 August 2020, Library of the Apostolic Palace

Notes for group leaders and catechists

These questions are intended to guide reflection, both as personal meditation and group reflection – prayer groups, parishes, catechism, ecumenical or volunteering groups, or any group of people of good will that cares about the destiny of humanity and our common home. In the latter case, depending on COVID regulations in your area,

---

[6] See *EG*, 183.

you could hold the reflection either in person, or online. We suggest that you ask each member of the group to read the weekly Catechesis before the meeting, or watch the video, so that they have time to think carefully before they meet. You could also give them the questions for reflection in advance. You don't have to answer all the questions, it will depend on how much time you have, and what strikes you as most important.

At the beginning of the session, allow some time for prayer, and conclude the reflections with another prayer.

CATECHESIS REFLECTIONS

1. What word or phrase most spoke to you when you read this text?

2. What signs of hope can you see in your life and in the life of your community at the moment? Where do you see compassion and care in action?

3. What challenges do you think your local community is facing at the moment?

4. Pope Francis suggests that the world needs healing. In what ways could you, your family, your friends and your community help heal our world? Think of one or two concrete ideas.

5. Pope Francis lists a number of key principles: the principle of the dignity of the person, the principle of the common good, the principle of the preferential option for the poor, the principle of the universal destination of goods, the principle of the solidarity, of subsidiarity, the principle of the care for our common home. Which of these principles are you most familiar with? Which ones are you most looking forward to finding out more about?

6. What changes would most help to bring about a better world? For example, more respect for nature; less environmental damage; better jobs for all; a universal basic income for everybody?

7. What does it mean for our attitudes towards other people to realise that we are all members of one human family?

DIGNITY AND FAITH

Dear brothers and sisters, good morning!

The pandemic has highlighted how vulnerable and interconnected everyone is. If we do not take care of one another, starting with the least, with those who are most impacted, including creation, we cannot heal the world.

Commendable is the effort of so many people who have been offering evidence of human and Christian love for neighbour, dedicating themselves to the sick even at the risk of their own health. They are heroes! However, the coronavirus is not the only disease to be fought, but rather, the pandemic has shed light on broader social ills. One of these is a distorted view of the person, a perspective that ignores her dignity and relational nature. At times we look at others as objects, to be used and discarded. In reality this type of perspective blinds and fosters an individualistic and aggressive throw-away culture, which transforms the human being into a consumer good.[1]

---

[1] Cf. *EG*, 53; *LS*, **22.**

In the light of faith we know, instead, that God looks at a man and a woman in another manner. He created us not as objects but as people who are loved and capable of loving; He has created us in His image and likeness (see *Gen* 1:27). In this way He has given us a unique dignity, calling us to live in communion with Him, in communion with our sisters and our brothers, with respect for all creation. In communion, in harmony, we might say. Creation is the harmony in which we are called to live. And in this communion, in this harmony that is communion, God gives us the ability to procreate and safeguard life (see *Gen* 1:28-29), to till and keep the land (see *Gen* 2:15).[2] It is clear that one cannot procreate and safeguard life without harmony; it will be destroyed.

We have an example of that individualistic perspective, that which is not harmony, in the Gospels, in the request made to Jesus by the mother of the disciples James and John (cf. *Mt* 20:20-38). She wanted her sons to sit at the right and the left of the new king. But Jesus proposes another type of vision: that of service and of giving one's life for others, and

---

[2] *LS*, 67.

He confirms it by immediately restoring sight to two blind men and making them His disciples (see *Mt* 20:29-34). Seeking to climb in life, to be superior to others, destroys harmony. It is the logic of dominion, of dominating others. Harmony is something else: it is service.

Therefore, let us ask the Lord to give us eyes attentive to our brothers and sisters, especially those who are suffering. As Jesus's disciples we do not want to be indifferent or individualistic. These are the two unpleasant attitudes that run counter to harmony. Indifferent: I look the other way. Individualist: looking out only for one's own interest. The harmony created by God asks that we look at others, the needs of others, the problems of others, in communion. We want to recognise the human dignity in every person, whatever his or her race, language or condition might be. Harmony leads you to recognise human dignity, that harmony created by God, with humanity at the centre.

The Second Vatican Council emphasises that this dignity is inalienable, because it "was created 'to the image of God'".[3] It lies at the foundation of all social life and determines its

---

[3] Pastoral Constitution *Gaudium et Spes* [*GS*], 12.

operative principles. In modern culture, the closest reference to the principle of the inalienable dignity of the person is the Universal Declaration of Human Rights, which Saint John Paul II defined as a "milestone on the long and difficult path of the human race",[4] and as "one of the highest expressions of the human conscience".[5] Rights are not only individual, but also social; they are of peoples, nations.[6] The human being, indeed, in his or her personal dignity, is a social being, created in the image of God, One and Triune. We are social beings; we need to live in this social harmony, but when there is selfishness, our outlook does not reach others, the community, but focuses on ourselves, and this makes us ugly, nasty and selfish, destroying harmony.

This renewed awareness of the dignity of every human being has serious social, economic and political implications. Looking at our brother and sister and the whole of creation as a gift received from the love of the

---

[4] *Address to the General Assembly of the United Nations* (2 October 1979).

[5] *Address to the General Assembly of the United Nations* (5 October 1995).

[6] Cf. *CSDC*, 157.

Father inspires attentive behaviour, care and wonder. In this way the believer, contemplating his or her neighbour as a brother or sister, and not as a stranger, looks at him or her compassionately and empathetically, not contemptuously or with hostility. Contemplating the world in the light of faith, with the help of grace, we strive to develop our creativity and enthusiasm in order to resolve the ordeals of the past. We understand and develop our abilities as responsibilities that arise from this faith,[7] as gifts from God to be placed at the service of humanity and of creation.

While we all work for a cure for a virus that strikes everyone without distinction, faith exhorts us to commit ourselves seriously and actively to combat indifference in the face of violations of human dignity. This culture of indifference that accompanies the throwaway culture: things that do not affect me, do not interest me. Faith always requires that we let ourselves be healed and converted from our individualism, whether personal or collective; party individualism, for example.

May the Lord "restore our sight" so as to rediscover what it means to be members

---

[7] *Ibid.*

of the human family. And may this sight be translated into concrete actions of compassion and respect for every person and of care and safeguarding of our common home.

General Audience, 12 August 2020, Library of the Apostolic Palace

CATECHESIS REFLECTIONS

1. What word or phrase most spoke to you when you read this text?

2. Do you know anyone you would describe as a hero — someone who has gone the extra mile to help others during this pandemic? What did they do?

3. How would you describe the difference between an individualistic culture and a culture of community? Could you give an example?

4. What would have to change before we could live in a way that respects the dignity of creation? What changes could you make in your own life that would reduce the everyday destruction of the environment?

5. Which groups of people in your country experience discrimination and prejudice? For example, how well does your country

treat refugees? Or homeless people? How could we better follow the example of Jesus in the ways that we treat others?

6. Who is your neighbour? How can you best respond to Pope Francis' words, and increase harmony in your own neighbourhood?

7. What concrete actions could you take as a community to show compassion towards those in need, locally and globally? And what could you do to show your care for our common home, the earth?

Option for the Poor and Love

Dear brothers and sisters, good day!

The pandemic has exposed the plight of the poor and the great inequality that reigns in the world. And the virus, while it does not distinguish between people, has found, in its devastating path, great inequalities and discrimination. And it has exacerbated them!

The response to the pandemic is therefore dual. On the one hand, it is essential to find a cure for this small but terrible virus, which has brought the whole world to its knees. On the other, we must also cure a larger virus, that of social injustice, inequality of opportunity, marginalisation, and the lack of protection for the weakest. In this dual response for healing there is a choice that, according to the Gospel, cannot be lacking: the *preferential option for the poor.*[1] And this is not a political option; nor is it an ideological option, a party option... no. The preferential option for the poor is at the centre of the Gospel. And the first to do this was Jesus; we heard this in the reading from the Letter to the Corin-

---

[1] See *EG*, 195.

thians which was read at the beginning. Since He was rich, He made Himself poor to enrich us. He made Himself one of us and for this reason, at the centre of the Gospel, there is this option, at the centre of Jesus' proclamation. Christ Himself, Who is God, despoiled Himself, making Himself similar to men; and he chose not a life of privilege, but he chose the condition of a servant (cf. *Phil* 2:6-7). He annihilated Himself by making Himself a servant. He was born into a humble family and worked as a craftsman. At the beginning of His preaching, He announced that in the Kingdom of God the poor are blessed (cf. *Mt* 5:3; *Lk* 6:20).[2] He stood among the sick, the poor, the excluded, showing them God's merciful love.[3] And many times He was judged an impure man because He went to the sick, to lepers… and this made people impure, according to the law of the age. And He took risks to be near to the poor.

Therefore, Jesus' followers recognise themselves by their closeness to the poor, the little ones, the sick and the imprisoned, the excluded and the forgotten, those without food

---

[2] *EG*, 197.
[3] Cf. CCC, 2444.

and clothing (cf. *Mt* 25:31-36).[4] We can read that famous protocol by which we will all be judged, we will all be judged. It is Matthew, chapter 25. This is a *key criterion of Christian authenticity* (cf. *Gal* 2:10).[5] Some mistakenly think that this preferential love for the poor is a task for the few, but in reality it is the mission of the Church as a whole, as Saint John Paul II said.[6] "Each individual Christian and every community is called to be an instrument of God for the liberation and promotion of the poor society".[7]

Faith, hope and love necessarily push us towards this preference for those most in need,[8] which goes beyond necessary assistance.[9] Indeed it implies walking together, letting ourselves be evangelised by them, who know the suffering Christ well, letting ourselves be "infected" by their experience of salvation, by their wisdom and by their creativity.[10] Sharing with the poor means mutual

---

[4] *Ibid.*, 2443.

[5] *EG*, 195.

[6] Cf. *SRS*, 42.

[7] *EG*, 187.

[8] See CONGREGATION FOR THE DOCTRINE OF THE FAITH, *Instruction on some aspects of "Liberation Theology"*, (1984), chap. V.

[9] Cf. *EG*, 198.

[10] See *ibid.*

enrichment. And, if there are unhealthy social structures that prevent them from dreaming of the future, we must work together to heal them, to change them.[11] And we are led to this by the love of Christ, Who loved us to the extreme (see *Jn* 13:1), and reaches the boundaries, the margins, the existential frontiers. Bringing the peripheries to the centre means focusing our life on Christ, Who "made Himself poor" for us, to enrich us "by His poverty" (2 *Cor* 8:9),[12] as we have heard.

We are all worried about the social consequences of the pandemic. All of us. Many people want to return to normality and resume economic activities. Certainly, but this "normality" should not include social injustices and the degradation of the environment. The pandemic is a crisis, and we do not emerge from a crisis the same as before: either we come out of it better, or we come out of it worse. We must come out of it better, to counter social injustice and environmental damage. Today we have an opportunity to build something different. For example, we can nurture

---

[11] See *ibid.*, 195.

[12] BENEDICT XVI, *Address at the Inaugural Session of the Fifth General Conference of the Bishops of Latin America and the Caribbean* (13 May 2007).

an economy of the integral development of the poor, and not of providing assistance. By this I do not wish to condemn assistance: aid is important. I am thinking of the voluntary sector, which is one of the best structures of the Italian Church. Yes, aid does this, but we must go beyond this, to resolve the problems that lead us to provide aid. An economy that does not resort to remedies that in fact poison society, such as profits not linked to the creation of dignified jobs.[13] This type of profit is dissociated from the real economy, that which should bring benefits to the common people,[14] and in addition is at times indifferent to the damage inflicted to our common home. The preferential option for the poor, this ethical-social need that comes from God's love,[15] inspires us to conceive of and design an economy where people, and especially the poorest, are at the centre. And it also encourages us to plan the treatment of viruses by prioritising those who are most in need. It would be sad if, for the vaccine for Covid-19, priority were to be given to the richest! It would be sad if this vaccine were to become the property of

---

[13] See *EG*, 204.
[14] See *LS*, 109.
[15] Cf. *ibid.*, 158.

this nation or another, rather than universal
and for all. And what a scandal it would be if
all the economic assistance we are observing
— most of it with public money — were to
focus on rescuing those industries that do not
contribute to the inclusion of the excluded,
the promotion of the least, the common good
or the care of creation.[16] There are criteria for
choosing which industries should be helped:
those which contribute to the inclusion of the
excluded, to the promotion of the last, to the
common good and the care of creation. Four
criteria.

If the virus were to intensify again in a
world that is unjust to the poor and vulnerable, then we must change this world. Following the example of Jesus, the doctor of integral divine love, that is, of physical, social and
spiritual healing (cf. *Jn* 5:6-9) — like the healing worked by Jesus — we must act now, to
heal the epidemics caused by small, invisible
viruses, and to heal those caused by the great
and visible social injustices. I propose that
this be done by starting from the love of God,
placing the peripheries at the centre and the
last in first place. Do not forget that protocol
by which we will be judged, Matthew, chap-

____

¹⁶ *Ibid.*

ter 25. Let us put it into practice in this recovery from the epidemic. And starting from this tangible love — as the Gospel says, there — anchored in hope and founded in faith, a healthier world will be possible. Otherwise, we will come out of the crisis worse. May the Lord help us, and give us the strength to come out of it better, responding to the needs of today's world. Thank you.

General Audience, 19 August 2020, Library of the Apostolic Palace

Catechesis Reflections

1. What word or phrase most spoke to you when you read this text?
2. What have you seen this week that is beautiful? Have you seen any examples of people helping out others?
3. In what ways do you think COVID-19 has made inequalities more obvious, and in what ways made them even worse? What negative impacts can you see on the lives of people living in poverty?
4. What is it that keeps people who live in poverty from being able to realise their dreams for the future? For example, is

good healthcare and education available to everyone in your country, rich and poor? Does everyone have somewhere safe and affordable to live?

5. What does it look like to take the side of the poor? Can you speak of a time when you took the side of the poor, or when you saw someone else do that? Who are the poor? Can you think of any saints who were particularly close to the poor?

6. What is it that makes a job 'dignified?' What conditions make a job less dignified?

7. How can you, your family and your group contribute to healing the world? What would it look like to follow Jesus' example by being close to the poor and outcast? What does your community already do to support the poorest and most excluded?

THE UNIVERSAL DESTINATION OF GOODS AND THE VIRTUE OF HOPE

Dear Brothers and Sisters, Good morning!

In the face of the pandemic and its social consequences, many risk losing hope. In this time of uncertainty and anguish, I invite everyone to welcome the gift of *hope* that comes from Christ. It is He who helps us navigate the tumultuous waters of sickness, death and injustice, which do not have the last word over our final destination.

The pandemic has exposed and aggravated social problems, above all that of inequality. Some people can work from home, while this is impossible for many others. Certain children, notwithstanding the difficulties involved, can continue to receive an academic education, while this has been abruptly interrupted for many, many others. Some powerful nations can issue money to deal with the crisis, while this would mean mortgaging the future for others.

These symptoms of inequality reveal a social illness; it is a virus that comes from a sick economy. And we must say it simply: the economy is sick. It has become ill. It is the fruit of unequal economic growth — this is the

illness: the fruit of unequal economic growth
— that disregards fundamental human values.
In today's world, a few wealthy people possess
more than all the rest of humanity. I will repeat
this so that it makes us think: a few wealthy
people, a small group, possess more than all
the rest of humanity. This is pure statistics.
This is an injustice that cries out to heaven! At
the same time, this economic model is indifferent to the damage inflicted on our common
home. Care is not being taken of our common
home. We are close to exceeding many limits
of our wonderful planet, with serious and irre-
versible consequences: from the loss of biodiversity and climate change to rising sea levels
and the destruction of the tropical forests. Social inequality and environmental degradation
go together and have the same root:[1] the sin of
wanting to possess and wanting to dominate
over one's brothers and sisters, of wanting to
possess and dominate nature and God himself.
But this is not the design for creation.

"In the beginning God entrusted the
earth and its resources to the common stew-
ardship of mankind to take care of them".[2]
God has called us to dominate the earth in his

---

[1] Cf. *LS*, 101.
[2] *CCC*, 2402.

name (cf. *Gen* 1:28), tilling it and keeping it like a garden, everyone's garden (cf. *Gen* 2:15). "'Tilling' refers to cultivating, ploughing or working, while 'keeping' means caring, protecting, overseeing and preserving".[3] But be careful not to interpret this as a carte blanche to do whatever you want with the earth. No. There exists a "relationship of mutual responsibility"[4] between ourselves and nature. A relationship of mutual responsibility between ourselves and nature. We receive from creation and we give back in return. "Each community can take from the bounty of the earth whatever it needs for subsistence, but it also has the duty to protect the earth".[5] It goes both ways.

In fact, the earth "was here before us and it has been given to us",[6] it has been given by God "for the whole human race".[7] And therefore it is our duty to make sure that its fruit reaches everyone, not just a few people. And this is a key element of our relationship with earthly goods. As the Fathers of the Second Vatican Council recalled, they said: "Man should regard the external things that he le-

---

[3] *LS*, 67.
[4] *Ibid.*
[5] *Ibid.*
[6] *Ibid.*
[7] *CCC*, 2402.

gitimately possesses not only as his own but also as common in the sense that they should be able to benefit not only him but also others".[8] In fact, "the ownership of any property makes its holder a steward of Providence, with the task of making it fruitful and communicating its benefits to others".[9] We are administrators of the goods, not masters. Administrators. "Yes, but the good is mine": that is true, it is yours, but to administer it, not to possess it selfishly for yourself.

To ensure that what we possess brings value to the community, "political authority has the right and duty to regulate the legitimate exercise of the right to ownership for the sake of the common good".[10] The "subordination of private property to the *universal destination of goods*, [...] is a golden rule of social conduct and the first principle of the whole ethical and social order".[11]

Property and money are instruments that can serve mission. However, we easily transform them into ends, whether individu-

---

[8] *GS*, 69.

[9] *CCC*, 2404.

[10] *Ibid.*, 2406. Cf. *GS*, 71; *SRS*, 42; Encyclical Letter *Centesimus Annus* [*CA*], 40,48.

[11] *LS*, 93, Cf. S. JOHN PAUL II, Encyclical Letter *Laborem exercens* [*LE*], 19.

al or collective. And when this happens, essential human values are affected. The *homo sapiens* is deformed and becomes a species of *homo œconomicus* — in a detrimental sense — a species of man that is individualistic, calculating and domineering. We forget that, being created in the image and likeness of God, we are social, creative and solidary beings with an immense capacity to love. We often forget this. In fact, from among all the species, we are the beings who are the most cooperative and we flourish in community, as is seen well in the experience of the saints. There is a saying in Spanish that inspired me to write this phrase. It says: "*Florecemos en racimo, como los santos*": we flourish in community, as is seen well in the experience of the saints.[12]

When the obsession to possess and dominate excludes millions of persons from having primary goods; when economic and technological inequality are such that the social fabric is torn; and when dependence on unlimited material progress threatens our common home, then we cannot stand by and watch. No, this is distressing. We cannot stand by and watch!

---

[12] "*Florecemos en racimo, como los santos*" (We bloom in clusters, like the saints): a popular expression in Spanish.

With our gaze fixed on Jesus (cf. *Heb* 12:2) and with the certainty that His love is operative through the community of His disciples, we must act all together, in the hope of generating something different and better. Christian hope, rooted in God, is our anchor. It moves the will to share, strengthening our mission as disciples of Christ, who shared everything with us.

The first Christian communities understood this. They lived difficult times, like us. Aware that they formed one heart and one soul, they put all of their goods in common, bearing witness to Christ's abundant grace in them (cf. *Acts* 4:32-35). We are experiencing a crisis. The pandemic has put us all in crisis. But let us remember that after a crisis a person is not the same. We come out of it better, or we come out of it worse. This is our option. After the crisis, will we continue with this economic system of social injustice and depreciating care for the environment, for creation, for our common home? Let's think about this. May the Christian communities of the 21st century recuperate this reality — care for creation and social justice: they go together —, thus bearing witness to the Lord's Resurrection. If we take care of the goods that the Creator gives us, if we put what we possess in common in such a way that no one would be lacking, then we would truly inspire hope to regenerate a more healthy and equal world.

And in conclusion, let us think about the children. Read the statistics: how many children today are dying of hunger because of a non good distribution of riches, because of the economic system as I said above; and how many children today do not have the right to education for the same reason. May this image of children in want due to hunger and the lack of education help us understand that after this crisis we must come out of it better. Thank you.

General Audience, 26 August 2020, Library of the Apostolic Palace

CATECHESIS REFLECTIONS

1. What word or phrase most spoke to you when you read this text?
2. Can you think of a time when you have shared something with someone else? How did you feel?
3. How do you feel about this statistic – that just a few people own more than all of the rest of humanity? What ideas do you have that would change this, so that more people could have enough of what they need to live on?

4. Are there any local signs, in your region or in your country, of environmental damage? Air pollution? Do you have clean water? Have you seen signs of climate change – for example, floods, droughts, or more damaging storms?

5. Who do you think of as rich? Is it someone who owns their own house? Someone who has more than one house? Someone who drives a fast car? How much would you need to earn in order to be rich in your country? How much do you need to earn just to get by?

6. What is a good example of sharing in your community? For example, have you set up a food bank? Could you offer a job to someone who is unemployed? Could you offer a room to an asylum seeker, or a free shower for a homeless person? What are your ideas?

7. In what way does caring for creation and bringing about social justice witness to the Lord's Resurrection? Is caring for creation and feeding hungry children a good way of letting people know about the love of Christ? What other ways are there? Which ways do you think have the most impact?

Solidarity and the Virtue of Faith

Dear Brothers and Sisters, good morning!

After many months, we meet each other again face to face, not screen to screen. Face to face. This is good! The current pandemic has highlighted our interdependence: we are all connected to each other, for better or for worse. Therefore, to emerge from this crisis better than before, we have to do so together; together, not alone. Together. Not alone, because it cannot be done. Either it is done together, or it is not done. We must do it together, all of us, in *solidarity*. I would like to underline this word today: *solidarity*.

As a human family we have our common origin in God; we live in a common home, the garden-planet, the earth where God placed us; and we have a common destination in Christ. But when we forget all this, our *interdependence* becomes *dependence* of some on others — we lose this harmony of interdependence and solidarity — increasing inequality and marginalization; the social fabric is weakened and the environment deteriorates. It's always the same way of acting.

Therefore, the *principle of solidarity* is now more necessary than ever, as Saint John Paul II taught.[1] In an interconnected world, we experience what it means to live in the same "global village"; this expression is beautiful. The big wide world is none other than a global village, because everything is interconnected, but we do not always transform this *interdependence* into *solidarity*. There is a long journey between interdependence and solidarity. The selfishness — of individuals, nations and of groups with power — and ideological rigidities instead sustain "structures of sin".[2]

"The word 'solidarity' is a little worn and at times poorly understood, but it refers to something more than a few sporadic acts of generosity". Much more! "It presumes the creation of a new mindset which thinks in terms of community and the priority of the life of all over the appropriation of goods by a few".[3] This is what "solidarity" means. It is not merely a question of helping others — it is good to do so, but it is more than that — it is

---

[1] Cf. *SRS*, 38-40.
[2] *Ibid.*, 36.
[3] *EG*, 188.

a matter of justice.[4] Interdependence, to be in solidarity and to bear fruit, needs strong roots in humanity and in nature, created by God; it needs respect for faces and for the land.

The Bible, from the very beginning, warns us [of this]. Let us think of the account of the Tower of Babel (cf. *Gen* 11:1-9), which describes what happens when we try to reach heaven — our destination — ignoring our bond with humanity, with creation and with the Creator. It is a figure of speech. This happens every time that someone wants to climb up and up, without taking others into consideration. Just myself. Let us think about the tower. We build towers and skyscrapers, but we destroy community. We unify buildings and languages, but we mortify cultural wealth. We want to be masters of the Earth, but we ruin biodiversity and ecological balance. In another audience I told you about those fishermen from San Benedetto del Tronto, who came this year, and said: "We have taken 24 tonnes of waste out of the sea, half of which was plastic". Just think! These people have the spirit to catch fish, yes, but also the refuse, and to take it out of the water to clean

---

[4] Cf. CCC, 1938-1949.

up the sea. But this [pollution] is ruining the earth — not having solidarity with the earth, which is a gift — and the ecological balance.

I remember a medieval account that describes this "Babel syndrome", which occurs when there is no solidarity. This medieval account says that, during the building of the tower, when a man fell — they were slaves — and died, no one said anything, or at best, "Poor thing, he made a mistake and he fell". Instead, if a brick fell, everyone complained. And if someone was to blame, he was punished. Why? Because a brick was costly to make, to prepare, to fire…. It took time and work to produce a brick. A brick was worth more than a human life. Let us each, think about what happens today. Unfortunately, something like this can happen nowadays too. When shares fall in the financial markets — we have seen it in the newspapers in these days — all the agencies report the news. Thousands of people fall due to hunger and poverty and no one talks about it.

Pentecost is diametrically opposite to Babel (cf. *Acts* 2:1-3), as we heard at the beginning of the audience. The Holy Spirit, descending from above like wind and fire, sweeps over the community closed up in the Cenacle, infuses it with the power of God, and inspires it to go out and announce the Lord Jesus to everyone. The Spirit creates unity in diversity; he creates harmony. In the account of the Tower of Babel, there was no harmony; only pressing forward in order to earn. There, people were simply instruments, mere "manpower", but here, in Pentecost, each one of us is an instrument, but a community instrument that participates fully in building up the community. Saint Francis of Assisi knew this well, and inspired by the Spirit, he gave all people, or rather, creatures, the name of brother or sister.[5] Even brother wolf, remember.

With Pentecost, God makes himself present and inspires the *faith* of the community *united in diversity and in solidarity*. Diversity and solidarity united in harmony, this is the way. A diversity in solidarity possesses "antibodies" that ensure that the singularity of each person — which is a gift, unique and unrepeatable — does not become sick with individualism, with selfishness. Diversity in solidarity also possesses antibodies that heal social structures and processes that have degenerated into systems of injustice, systems of

---

[5] Cf. *LS*, 11; cf. SAINT BONAVENTURE, *Legenda maior*, VIII, 6: ff 1145.

oppression.[6] Therefore, solidarity today is the road to take towards a post-pandemic world, towards the healing of our interpersonal and social ills. There is no other way. Either we go forward on the path of solidarity, or things will worsen. I want to repeat this: one does not emerge from a crisis the same as before. The pandemic is a crisis. We emerge from a crisis either better or worse than before. It is up to us to choose. And solidarity is, indeed, a way of coming out of the crisis better, not with superficial changes, with a fresh coat of paint so everything looks fine. No. Better!

In the midst of crises, a *solidarity* guided by *faith* enables us to translate the love of God in our globalized culture, not by building towers or walls — and how many walls are being built today! — that divide, but then collapse, but by interweaving communities and sustaining processes of growth that are truly human and solid. And to do this, solidarity helps. I would like to ask a question: do I think of the needs of others? Everyone, answer in your heart.

In the midst of crises and tempests, the Lord calls to us and invites us to reawaken

---

6 Cf. *CSDC*, 192.

and activate this solidarity capable of giving solidity, support and meaning to these hours in which everything seems to be wrecked. May the creativity of the Holy Spirit encourage us to generate new forms of familiar hospitality, fruitful fraternity and universal solidarity. Thank you.

General Audience, 2 September 2020, San Damaso courtyard

Catechesis Reflections

1. What word or phrase most spoke to you when you read this text?

2. Can you think of good examples of ways in which you or your group act in solidarity – either locally, or globally? For example, by supporting Caritas, or by campaigning for cycle paths or creating playgrounds for disadvantaged children.

3. In what ways are you connected to people in other parts of the world? For example, do you buy fruit from the Caribbean, or clothes made in Bangladesh? How could you move from being connected, to being in solidarity? What is the difference?

4. What does it mean to be in solidarity with the rest of creation? Cleaning up plastic waste is a good thing. But is there more we could do?

5. What do you think going forward on the path of solidarity looks like? What changes would it mean? Are we ready to give up all the advantages of a selfish way of life in order to help others? Do we know anyone who is already walking on this path of solidarity and could be an example to us?

6. Why do you think so many walls are being built today? What are people afraid of? How could we help people to overcome their fears and break down the walls?

7. Do you remember the story of the Tower of Babel? (*Gen* 11, 1-9). What can it teach us about solidarity?

Love and the Common Good

Dear Brothers and Sisters, good morning!

The crisis we are living due to the pandemic is affecting everyone; we will emerge from it for the better if we all seek the *common good* together; the contrary is we will emerge for the worse. Unfortunately, we see partisan interests emerging. For example, some would like to appropriate possible solutions for themselves, as in the case of vaccines, to then sell them to others. Some are taking advantage of the situation to instigate divisions: by seeking economic or political advantages, generating or exacerbating conflicts. Others simply are not interested themselves in the suffering of others, they pass by and go their own way (see *Lk* 10:30-32). They are the devotees of Pontius Pilate, washing their hands of others' suffering.

The Christian response to the pandemic and to the consequent socio-economic crisis is based on *love*, above all, the love of God who always precedes us (see *1 Jn* 4:19). He loves us first, He always precedes us in love and in solutions. He loves us unconditionally, and when we welcome this divine love, then we can respond similarly. I love not only those who love me — my family, my friends, my group — but I also love those who do not love me, I also love those who do not know me or who are strangers, and even those who make me suffer or whom I consider enemies (see *Mt* 5:44). This is Christian wisdom, this is how Jesus acted. And the highest point of holiness, let's put it that way, is to love one's enemies which is not easy, it is not easy. Certainly, to love everyone, including enemies, is difficult — I would say it is even an art! But an art that can be learned and improved. True love that makes us fruitful and free is always expansive, and true love is not only expansive, it is inclusive. This love cares, heals and does good. How many times a caress does more good than many arguments; a caress, we can think, of pardon instead of many arguments to defend oneself. It is inclusive love that heals.

So, *love* is not limited to the relationship between two or three people, or to friends or to family, it goes beyond. It comprises civil and political relationships,[1] including a relationship with nature.[2] Since we are social and political beings, one of the highest expressions

---

[1] See CCC, 1907-1912.
[2] See LS, 231.

of love is specifically social and political which is decisive to human development and in order to face any type of crisis.[3] We know that love makes families and friendships flourish; but it is good to remember that it also makes social, cultural, economic and political relationships flourish, allowing us to construct a "civilisation of love", as Saint Paul VI used to love to say[4] and, in turn, Saint John Paul II. Without this inspiration the egotistical, indifferent, throwaway culture prevails — that is to discard anything I do not like, whom I cannot love or those who seem to me to not to be useful in society. Today at the entrance, a married couple said to us: "Pray for me (us) because we have a disabled son". I asked: "How old is he?" "He is pretty old". "And what do you do?" "We accompany him, help him". All of their lives as parents for that disabled son. This is love. And the enemies, the adversarial politicians, according to our opinion, seem to be "disabled" politicians, socially, but they seem to be that way. Only God knows if they are truly thus or not. But we must love them, we must dialogue, we must build this civili-

---

[3] *Ibid.*, 231.

[4] *Message for the X World Day of Peace, 1 January 1977: AAS* 68 (1976), 709.

sation of love, this political and social civilisation of the unity of all humanity. Otherwise, wars, divisions, envy, even wars in families: because inclusive love is social, it is familial, it is political… love pervades everything.

The coronavirus is showing us that each person's true good is a common good, not only individual, and, *vice versa*, the common good is a true good for the person.[5] If a person only seeks his or her own good, that person is egotistical. Instead, the person is kinder, nobler, when his or her own good is open to everyone, when it is shared. Health, in addition to being an individual good, is also a public good. A healthy society is one that takes care of everyone's health, of all.

A virus that does not recognise barriers, borders, or cultural or political distinctions must be faced with a *love* without barriers, borders or distinctions. This love can generate social structures that encourage us to share rather than to compete, that allow us to include the most vulnerable and not to cast them aside, that help us to express the best in our human nature and not the worst. True love does not know the throwaway culture, it does

---

[5] See CCC, 1905-1906.

not know what it is. In fact, when we love and generate creativity, when we generate trust and solidarity, it is then that concrete initiatives emerge for the common good.[6] And this is valid at both the level of the smallest and largest communities, as well as at the international level. What is done in the family, what is done in the neighbourhood, what is done in the village, what is done in the large cities and internationally is the same, it is the same seed that grows, grows, grows and bears fruit. If you in your family, in your neighbourhood start out with envy, with battles, there will be war in the end. Instead, if you start out with love, to share love, forgiveness, there will be love and forgiveness for everyone.

Conversely, if the solutions for the pandemic bear the imprint of egoism, whether it be by persons, businesses or nations, we may perhaps emerge from the coronavirus crisis, but certainly not from the human and social crisis that the virus has brought to light and accentuated. Therefore, be careful not to build on sand (see *Mt* 7:21-27)! To build a healthy, inclusive, just and peaceful society we must do so on the rock of the common good.[7] The

---

[6] See *SRS*, 38.
[7] *Ibid.*, 10.

common good is a rock. And this is everyone's task, not only that of a few specialists.
Saint Thomas Aquinas used to say that the
promotion of the common good is a duty of
justice that falls on each citizen. Every citizen
is responsible for the common good. And for
Christians, it is also a mission. As Saint Ignatius of Loyola taught, to direct our daily efforts
toward the common good is a way of receiv-
ing and spreading God's glory.

Unfortunately, politics does not often
have a good reputation, and we know why.
This is not to say that all politicians are bad,
no, I do not want to say this. I am only saying
that unfortunately, politics do not often have
a good reputation. Why? But it does not have
to resign itself to this negative vision, but instead react to it by showing in deeds that good
politics is possible, or rather that politics[8] that
puts the human person and the common good
at the center is a duty. If you read the history
of humanity you will find many holy politicians who trod this path. It is possible inso-
far as every citizen, and especially those who
assume social and political commitments and
positions, roots what they do in ethical prin-

---

[8] See *Message for World Day of Peace, 1 January
2019* (8 December 2018).

ciples and nurtures it with social and political love. Christians, in a particular way the laity, are called to give good example of this and can do it thanks to the virtue of charity, cultivating its intrinsic social dimension.

It is therefore time to improve our social love — I want to highlight this: our social love — with everyone's contribution, starting from our littleness. The common good requires everyone's participation. If everyone contributes his or her part, and if no one is left out, we can regenerate good relationships on the communitarian, national and international level and even in harmony with the environment.[9] Thus, through our gestures, even the most humble ones, something of the image of God we bear within us will be made visible, because God is the Trinity, God is love, God is love. This is the most beautiful definition of God that is in the Bible. The Apostle John, who loved Jesus so much, gives it to us. With His help, we can heal the world working, yes, all together for the common good, for everyone's common good. Thank you.

General Audience, 9 September 2020, San Damaso courtyard

---

[9] See *LS*, 236.

1. What word or phrase most spoke to you when you read this text?

2. What do you think is the difference between seeking the Common Good together and abiding by the wishes of the majority? Who loses out if you only think about the majority view?

3. Why should we, as Catholics or simply as people of good will, seek to overcome racism and other forms of discrimination?

4. In what ways would a society built on love look different from the society we have now? Can you think of any examples of civic and political love? For example, overcoming apartheid in South Africa.

5. Why does Pope Francis say that health care should not be limited to those who can pay for it? To what extent is the prevention of disease a public or community issue, rather than just a private issue?

6. In what ways could we use technology for the common good, rather than just for our own private interests?

7. How could we come together more as a community, overcome division, and start to rebuild trust so that we could begin to build a better world post-COVID? What would be your first steps?

Care of the Common Home and the Contemplative Dimension

Dear Brothers and Sisters, Good morning!

To emerge from a pandemic, we need to look after and care for each other. And we must support those who care for the weakest, the sick and the elderly. There is the tendency to cast the elderly aside, to abandon them: this is bad. These people – well defined by the Spanish term *cuidadores* (caretakers), those who take care of the sick – play an essential role in today's society, even if they often do not receive the recognition and recompense they deserve. Caring is a golden rule of our nature as human beings, and brings with it health and hope.[1] Taking care of those who are sick, of those who are in need, of those who are cast aside: this is a human and also Christian wealth.

We must also extend this care to our common home: to the earth and to every creature. All forms of life are interconnected,[2] and our health depends on that of the ecosystems

---

[1] Cf. *LS*, 70.
[2] Cf. *ibid.*, 137-138.

that God created and entrusted us to care for (cf. *Gen* 2:15). Abusing them, on the other hand, is a grave sin that damages, harms and sickens.[3] The best antidote against this misuse of our common home is contemplation.[4] But why? Isn't there a vaccine for this, for the care of our common home, so as not to set it aside? What is the antidote against the sickness of not taking care of our common home? It is contemplation. "If someone has not learned to stop and admire something beautiful, we should not be surprised if he or she treats everything as an object to be used and abused without scruple".[5] Also in terms of "disposable" objects. However, our common home, creation, is not a mere "resource". Creatures have a value in themselves and each one "reflects in its own way a ray of God's infinite wisdom and goodness".[6] This value and this ray of divine light must be discovered and, in order to discover it, we need to be silent; we need to listen; we need to contemplate. Contemplation also heals the soul.

---

[3] Cf. *ibid.*, 8; 66.
[4] Cf. *ibid.*, 85, 214.
[5] *Ibid.*, 215.
[6] *CCC*, 339.

Without contemplation, it is easy to fall prey to an unbalanced and arrogant anthropocentrism, the "I" at the centre of everything, which overinflates our role as human beings, positioning us as absolute rulers of all other creatures. A distorted interpretation of biblical texts on creation has contributed to this misinterpretation, which leads to the exploitation of the earth to the point of suffocating it. Exploiting creation: this is the sin. We believe we are at the centre, claiming to occupy God's place and so we ruin the harmony of creation, the harmony of God's plan. We become predators, forgetting our vocation as custodians of life. Of course, we can and must work the earth so as to live and to develop. But work is not synonymous with exploitation, and it is always accompanied by care: ploughing and protecting, tilling and keeping... This is our mission (cf. *Gen* 2:15). We cannot expect to continue to grow on a material level, without taking care of the common home that welcomes us. Our poorest brothers and sisters and our mother earth groan for the damage and injustice we have caused, and demand we take another course. They demand of us a conversion, a change of path; taking care of the earth too, of creation.

Therefore, it is important to recover the contemplative dimension, that is, to look at the earth, creation, as a gift, not as something to exploit for profit. When we contemplate, we discover in others and in nature something much greater than their usefulness. Here is the heart of the issue: contemplating is going beyond the usefulness of something. Contemplating the beautiful does not mean exploiting it: contemplating is free. We discover the intrinsic value of things given to them by God. As many spiritual masters have taught, the heavens, the earth, the sea, and every creature possess this iconic capacity, this mystical capacity to bring us back to the Creator and to communion with creation. For example, Saint Ignatius of Loyola, at the end of his Spiritual Exercises, invites us to carry out "Contemplation to attain love", that is, to consider how God looks at his creatures and to rejoice with them; to discover God's presence in his creatures and, with freedom and grace, to love and care for them.

Contemplation, which leads us to an attitude of care, is not a question of looking at nature from the outside, as if we were not immersed in it. But we are inside nature, we are part of nature. Rather, it is done from within, recognizing ourselves as part of creation, making us protagonists and not mere spectators of an amorphous reality that is only to be exploited. Those who contemplate in this way experience wonder not only at what they see, but also because they feel they are an integral part of this beauty; and they also feel called to guard it and to protect it. And there is one thing we must not forget: those who cannot contemplate nature and creation cannot contemplate people in their true wealth. And those who live to exploit nature end up exploiting people and treating them like slaves. This is a universal law. If you cannot contemplate nature it will be very difficult for you to contemplate people, the beauty of people, your brother, your sister.

Those who know how to contemplate will more easily set to work to change what produces degradation and damage to health. They will strive to educate and promote new habits of production and consumption, to contribute to a new model of economic growth that guarantees respect for our common home and respect for people. The contemplative in action tends to become a guardian of the environment: this is good! Each one of us should be a guardian of the environment, of the purity of the environment, seeking to combine ancestral knowledge of millennia-long cultures with new technical knowledge, so that our lifestyle may always be sustainable.

Lastly, *contemplating and caring*: these are two attitudes that show the way to correct and re-balance our relationship as human beings with creation. Oftentimes, our relationship with creation seems to be a relationship between enemies: destroying creation for our benefit. Exploiting creation for our profit. Let us not forget that this comes at a high price; let us not forget that Spanish saying: "God always forgives; we forgive sometimes; nature never forgives". Today I was reading in the newspaper about those two great glaciers in Antarctica, near the Amundsen Sea: they are about to fall. It will be terrible, because the sea level will rise and this will bring many, many difficulties and so much harm. And why? Because of global warming, not caring for the environment, not caring for our common home. On the other hand, when we have this relationship – let me say the word – 'fraternal' in the figurative sense with creation, we will become guardians of our common home, guardians of life and guardians of hope; we will safeguard the patrimony that God has entrusted to us so that future generations may enjoy it. And some may say: "But, I can get by like this". But the problem is not how you are going to manage today – this was said by a German theologian, a Protestant, a good man: Bonhoeffer – the problem is not how you manage today; the problem is: what will be the legacy, life for future generations? Let us think of our children, our grandchildren: what will we leave them if we exploit creation? Let us protect this path so we may become "guardians" of our common home, guardians of life and hope. Let us safeguard the heritage that God has entrusted to us so that future generations may enjoy it. I think especially of the indigenous peoples, to whom we all owe a debt of gratitude, also of penance, to repair the harm we have done to them. But I am also thinking of those movements, associations, popular groups, that are committed to protecting their territory with its natural and cultural values. These social realities are not always appreciated; and at times they are even obstructed, because they do not earn money. But in reality they contribute to a peaceful revolution: we might call it the "revolution of care". Contemplating so as to care, contemplating to protect, to protect ourselves, creation, our children, our grandchildren, and to protect the future. Contemplating to care for and to protect, and to leave a legacy to the future generation.

However this must not be delegated to others: this is the task of every human being. Each one of us can and must be a "guardian of the common home", capable of praising God for his creatures, and of contemplating creatures, and protecting them. Thank you.

General Audience, 16 September 2020, San Damaso courtyard

CATECHESIS REFLECTIONS

1. What word or phrase most spoke to you when you read this text?

2. What have you seen recently that has struck you with its beauty? Did you have time to stop and contemplate it? If not, what changes would you have to make to your lifestyle in order to develop a more contemplative approach?

3. In what ways do we treat other living creatures well? And are there examples of when we treat them badly, as if they were of no value?

4. Can you think of any local examples of how the earth is being exploited instead of cared for? What about globally?

5. In what ways could you and your community do more to protect nature? What do you do already? What would be one easy extra step?

6. How do you see the relationship between contemplation and action? Is one more important than the other?

7. As well as becoming 'guardians of our common home' yourself, what do you think are the best ways to encourage and invite others to join you?

Subsidiarity and the Virtue of Hope

Dear Brothers and Sisters, it does not seem that the weather is that great, but I wish you a good morning all the same!

To emerge better from a crisis like the current one, which is a health crisis and is, at the same time, a social, political and economic crisis, every one of us is called to assume responsibility for our own part, that is, to share the responsibility. We must respond not only as individual people, but also from the groups to which we belong, out of the roles we have in society, from our principles and, if we are believers, from our faith in God. Often, however, many people cannot participate in the reconstruction of the common good because they are marginalised, they are excluded or ignored; certain social groups do not succeed in making a contribution because they are economically or socially suffocated. In some societies, many people are not free to express their own faith and their own values, their own ideas: if they express them freely, they are put in jail. Elsewhere, especially in the western world, many people repress their own ethical or religious convictions. This is no way to emerge from the crisis, or at least to emerge from it better. We will emerge from it worse.

So that we might be able to participate in the healing and regeneration of our peoples, it is only right that everyone should have the adequate resources to do so.[1] After the great economic depression of 1929, Pope Pius XI explained how important the *principle of subsidiarity* was.[2] This principle has a double movement: from top to bottom and from bottom to top. Perhaps we do not understand what this means, but it is a social principle that makes us more united. I will try to explain it.

On the one hand, and above all in moments of change, when single individuals, families, small associations and local communities are not capable of achieving primary objectives, it is then right that the highest levels of society, such as the State, should intervene to provide the necessary resources to progress. For example, because of the coronavirus lockdown, many people, families and economic entities found themselves, and still find themselves, in serious trouble. Thus, public institutions are trying to help through appropriate interven-

---

[1] See *CSDC*, 186.
[2] See Encyclical *Quadrasegimo anno*, 79-80.

tions, social economic, regarding health… this is their function, what they need to do.

On the other hand, however, society's leaders must respect and promote the intermediate or lower levels. In fact, the contribution of individuals, of families, of associations, of businesses, or every intermediary body, and even of the Church, is decisive. All of these, with their own cultural, religious, economic resources, or civil participation, revitalize and reinforce society.[3] That is, there is a collaboration from the top and the bottom from the State to the people, and from the bottom to the top, from the institutions of people to the top. And this is exactly how the principle of subsidiarity is exercised.

Everyone needs to have the possibility of assuming their own responsibility in the process of healing the society of which they are a part. When a project is launched that directly or indirectly touches certain social groups, these groups cannot be left out from participating – for example: "What do you do?" "I go to work with the poor". "Ah, how beautiful. And what do you do?" "I teach the poor, I tell the poor what they need to do".

---

[3] See *CSDC*, 185.

No, this doesn't work. The first step is to allow the poor to tell you how they live, what they need... Let everyone speak! And this is how the principle of subsidiarity works. We cannot leave out the participation of the people; their wisdom; the wisdom of the humbler groups cannot be set aside.[4] Unfortunately, this injustice happens often in those places where huge economic and geopolitical interests are concentrated, such as, for example, certain extractive activities in some areas of the planet.[5] The voices of the indigenous peoples, their culture and world visions are not taken into consideration. Today, this lack of respect of the *principle of subsidiarity* has spread like a virus. Let's think of the grand financial assistance measures enacted by States. The largest financial companies are listened to rather than the people or the ones who really move the economy. Multinational companies are listened to more than social movements. Putting it in everyday language, they listen more to the powerful than to the weak and this is not the way, it is not the human way, it is not the way that Jesus taught us, it is not how the principle of

---

[4] See Apostolic Exhortation *Querida Amazonia* [QA], 32; See *Quadrasegimo anno*, 79-80; See *LS*, 63.
[5] See *QA*, 9.14.

subsidiarity is implemented. Thus, we do not permit people to be "agents in their own redemption".[6] There is this motto in the collective unconscious of some politicians or some social workers: everything for the people, nothing with the people. From top to bottom without listening to the wisdom of the people, without activating the wisdom of the people in resolving problems, in this case to emerge from the crisis. Or let's think about the cure for the virus: the large pharmaceutical companies are listened to more than the healthcare workers employed on the front lines in hospitals or in refugee camps. This is not a good path. Everyone should be listened to, those who are at the top and those who are at the bottom, everyone.

To emerge better from a crisis, the *principle of subsidiarity* must be enacted, respecting the autonomy and the capacity to take initiative that everyone has, especially the least. All the parts of the body are necessary, as St Paul says, we've heard that those parts that may seem the weakest and least important, in reality are the most necessary (see *1 Cor* 12:22). In light of this image, we can say that the principle of subsidi-

---

[6] *Message for the 106th World Day of Migrants and Refugees 2020* (13 May 2020).

arity allows everyone to assume his or her own role for the healing and destiny of society. Implementing it, implementing the principle of subsidiarity gives *hope* in a healthier and more just future; let's construct this future together, aspiring to greater things, broadening our horizons and ideals.[7] Either we do it together, or it won't work. Either we work together to emerge from the crisis, all levels of society, or we will never emerge from it. It does not work that way. To emerge from the crisis does not mean to varnish over current situations so that they might appear more just. No. To emerge from the crisis means to change, and true change to which every contributes, all the persons that form a people. All the professions, all of them. And everything together, everyone in the community. If not everyone is contributing, the result will be negative.

In a previous catechesis we saw how *solidarity* – solidarity now – is the way out of the crisis: it unites us and allows us to find solid proposals for a healthier world. But this path of solidarity needs *subsidiarity*. Someone might say to me: "But, Father, today you are saying difficult things!" It's because of this that I am

---

[7] See *Discourse to students at the Fr. Félix Varela Cultural Center*, Havana – Cuba, 20 September 2015.

trying to explain what it means. Solidary, because we are taking the path of subsidiarity. In fact, there is no true solidarity without social participation, without the contribution of intermediary bodies: families, associations, cooperatives, small businesses, and other expressions of society. Everyone needs to contribute, everyone. This type of participation helps to prevent and to correct certain negative aspects of globalization and the actions of States, just as it is happening regarding the healing of people affected by the pandemic. These contributions "from the bottom" should be encouraged. How beautiful it is to see the volunteers during the crisis. The volunteers come from every part of society, volunteers who come from well-off families and those who come from poorer families. But everyone, everyone together to emerge. This is solidarity and this is the principle of subsidiarity.

During the lockdown, the spontaneous gesture of applauding, applause for doctors and nurses began as a sign of encouragement and hope. Many risked their lives and many gave their lives. Let's extend this applause to every member of the social body, to each and every one, for their precious contribution, no matter how small. "But can that person over there do?" "Listen to that person! Give the person space to work, consult him or her". Let's applaud the "cast-aways", those whom culture defines as those to be "thrown out", this throwaway culture – that is, let's applaud the elderly, children, persons with disability, let's applaud workers, all those who dedicate themselves to service. Everyone collaborating to emerge from the crisis. But let's not stop only at applauding. *Hope* is audacious, and so, let's encourage ourselves to dream big. Brothers and sisters, let's learn to dream big! Let's not be afraid to dream big, seeking the ideals of justice and social love that are born of hope. Let's not try to reconstruct the past, the past is the past, let's look forward to new things. The Lord's promise is: "I will make all things new" (*Is.* 43:19). Let's encourage ourselves to dream big, seeking those ideals, not trying to reconstruct the past, above all the past that was unjust and already ill.... Let's construct a future where the local and global dimensions mutually enrich each other – everyone can contribute, everyone must contribute their share, from their culture, from their philosophy, from their way of thinking – where the beauty and the wealth of smaller groups, even the groups that are cast aside, might flourish – because beauty is there too – and where those who have more dedicate themselves to service and give more to those who have less. Thank you.

General Audience, 23 September 2020, San Damaso courtyard

Catechesis Reflections

1. What word or phrase most spoke to you when you read this text?

2. Do you know the principle of "subsidiarity"? The Pope explains the exercise of this principle as "a collaboration from the top and the bottom from the State to the people, and from the bottom to the top, from the institutions of people to the top". Can you recall an example in which the state has helped a community in state of emergency in your country? Can you mention a couple of institutions born from private initiatives that help people or contribute to the common good where the State does not get to?

3. What did your government offer to help people in serious difficulties during lockdown? Was it sufficient? Too much? Did you hope for more help? And if so, what could have been done?

4. Who are the groups who are marginalised, excluded or ignored in your society? Who is excluded from top-level decision making? Is it Black and minority ethnic communities? Women? Immigrants and refugees? Low paid workers and unemployed people? How can we ensure that everyone's voice is heard when we make big decisions?

5. What have you, your family and your community been doing to help others during the pandemic? Which of your activities do you think were most helpful? What do you think stops more people from becoming involved in local community support?

6. Pope Francis suggests that big companies are listened to much more than ordinary workers and social movements. Can you think of any examples of this happening in your country? Can you think of any examples where those on the 'front line' of hospitals, care homes and refugee camps have been able to make their voices heard? How did they do it? What could we learn from them?

7. In what ways was the world already unfair before COVID? What would you like to bring back from the world before COVID and what would you like to change?

Preparing the Future Together with Jesus Who Saves and Heals

Dear Brothers and Sisters, good morning!

In recent weeks we have reflected together, in the light of the Gospel, on how to heal the world that is suffering from a malaise that the pandemic has highlighted and accentuated. The malaise was already there: the pandemic highlighted it more, it accentuated it. We have walked the paths of dignity, solidarity and subsidiarity, paths that are essential to promote human dignity and the common good. And as disciples of Jesus, we have proposed to follow in His steps, opting for the poor, rethinking the use of material goods and taking care of our common home. In the midst of the pandemic that afflicts us, we have anchored ourselves to the principles of the social doctrine of the Church, letting ourselves be guided by faith, by hope and by charity. Here we have found solid help so as to be transformers who dream big, who are not stopped by the meanness that divides and hurts, but who encourage the generation of a new and better world.

I hope this journey will not come to an end with this catechesis of mine, but rather that we may be able to continue to walk together, to "keep our eyes fixed on Jesus" (*Heb* 12:2), as we heard at the beginning; our eyes fixed on Jesus, who saves and heals the world. As the Gospel shows us, Jesus healed the sick of every type (see *Mt* 9:35), He gave sight to the blind, the word to the mute, hearing to the deaf. And when He cured diseases and physical infirmity, He also healed the spirit by forgiving sins, because Jesus always forgives, as well as "social pains" by including the marginalised (see *Catechism of the Catholic Church,* 1421). Jesus, who renews and reconciles every creature (see *2 Cor* 5.17; *Col* 1:19-20), gives us the gifts necessary to love and heal as He knew how to do (see *Lk* 10:1-9; *Jn* 15:9-17), to take care of all without distinction on the basis of race, language or nation.

So that this may truly happen, we need to contemplate and appreciate the beauty of every human being and every creature. We were conceived in the heart of God (see *Eph* 1:3-5). "Each of us is the result of a thought of God. Each of us is willed, each of us is loved, eachof us is necessary".[1] Furthermore, every creature has something to say to us about God the creator.[2] Acknowledging this truth and giving thanks for the intimate bonds in our universal communion with all people and all creatures activates "generous care, full of tenderness".[3] And it also helps us to recognise Christ present in our poor and suffering brothers and sisters, to encounter them and to listen to their cry and the cry of the earth that echoes it.[4]

Inwardly mobilised by these cries that demand of us another course,[5] that demand we change, we will be able to contribute to the restoration of relations with our gifts and capacities.[6] We will be able to regenerate society and not return to so-called "normality", which is an ailing normality, which was ailing before the pandemic: the pandemic highlighted it! "Now we return to normality": no, this will not do, because this normality was sick with injustice, inequality and environmental

---

[1] BENEDICT XVI, *Homily for the beginning of the Petrine ministry* (24 April 2005); see Encyclical *LS*, 65.
[2] See *LS*, 69, 239.
[3] *Ibid.*, 220.
[4] See *ibid.*, 49.
[5] See *ibid.*, 53.
[6] See *ibid.*, 19.

degradation. The normality to which we are called is that of the Kingdom of God, where "the blind see again, and the lame walk, those suffering from virulent skin-diseases are cleansed, and the deaf hear, the dead are raised to life and the good news is proclaimed to the poor" (*Mt* 11:5). And nobody plays dumb by looking the other way. This is what we have to do in order to change. In the normality of the Kingdom of God, there is bread for all and more to spare, social organisation is based on contributing, sharing and distributing, not on possessing, excluding and accumulating (see *Mt* 14:13-21).

The gesture that enables progress in a society, a family, a neighbourhood, or a city, all of them, is to give oneself, to give, which is not giving alms, but to give from the heart. A gesture that distances us from selfishness and the eagerness to possess. But the Christian way of doing this is not a mechanical way: it is a human way. We will never be able to emerge from the crisis that has been highlighted by the pandemic, mechanically, with new tools — which are very important, they allow us to move forward, and we must not be afraid of them — but knowing that even the most sophisticated means, able to do many things, are incapable of one thing:

tenderness. And tenderness is the very sign of Jesus' presence. Approaching others in order to walk together, to heal, to help, to sacrifice oneself for others.

So it is important, that normality of the Kingdom of God: there is bread for everyone, social organisation is based on contributing, sharing and distributing, with tenderness; not on possessing, excluding and accumulating. Because at the end of life, we will not take anything with us into the other life!

A small virus continues to cause deep wounds and to expose our physical, social and spiritual vulnerabilities. It has laid bare the great inequality that reigns in the world: inequality of opportunity, inequality of goods, inequality of access to health care, inequality of technology, education: millions of children cannot go to school, and so the list goes on. These injustices are neither natural nor inevitable. They are the work of man, they come from a model of growth detached from the deepest values. Food waste: with that waste one can feed others. And this has made many people lose hope and has increased uncertainty and anguish. That is why, to come out of the pandemic, we must find the cure not only for the *coronavirus* – which is important! – but also for the great human and socio-economic *viruses*. They must not be concealed or whitewashed so they cannot be seen. And certainly we cannot expect the economic model that underlies unfair and unsustainable development to solve our problems. It has not and will not, because it cannot do so, even though some false prophets continue to promise the "trickle-down" that never comes.[7] You have heard yourselves, the theory of the glass: it is important that the glass is full, and then overflows to the poor and to others, and they receive wealth. But there is a phenomenon: the glass starts to fill up and when it is almost full it grows, it grows and it grows, and never overflows. We must be careful.

We need to set to work urgently to generate good policies, to design systems of social organisation that reward participation, care and generosity, rather than indifference, exploitation and particular interests. We must go ahead with tenderness. A fair and equitable society is a healthier society. A participatory society — where the "last" are taken into account just like the "first" — strengthens communion. A society where diversity is

____

[7] *"Trickle-down effect"* in English, *"derrame"* in Spanish (see *EG*, 54).

respected is much more resistant to any kind of virus.

Let us place this healing journey under the protection of the Virgin Mary, Our Lady of Health. May she, who carried Jesus in her womb, help us to be trustful. Inspired by the Holy Spirit, we can work together for the Kingdom of God that Christ inaugurated in this world by coming among us. It is a Kingdom of light in the midst of darkness, of justice in the midst of so many outrages, of joy in the midst of so much pain, of healing and of salvation in the midst of sickness and death, of tenderness in the midst of hatred. May God grant us to "viralise" *love* and to "globalise" *hope* in the light of *faith*.

General Audience, 30 September 2020, San Damaso courtyard

CATECHESIS REFLECTIONS

1. What word or phrase most spoke to you when you read this text?

2. Which text from Scripture most ignites your passion to heal the world? Which parable or other gospel story really sets your heart on fire?

3. What would it mean in your own life to 'opt for the poor, rethink the use of goods, and care for creation'? What will be your first practical steps as you set out once more to follow in the footsteps of Jesus?

4. How do you feel when you read that you are 'wanted, loved and necessary?' What could you do to make sure that everyone knows that they are wanted, loved and necessary?

5. There is a lot of talk about a 'new normal'. Have you seen any signs that this new normal could be more just, more equal and more sustainable?

6. Pope Francis is suggesting that the old economic models and systems have not delivered what the poorest and most vulnerable need, nor have they protected God's beautiful creation. Can you imagine a new type of economic system? What would it need to deliver for you, for people in your community and for our wonderful and precious world?

7. At the end of this catechesis we ask for the protection of the Virgin Mary. What is your prayer for the world today?

INDEX